Poetry for Women

Book 2 of 4

BRIAN ALAN BILD

Poetry for Women
Book 2 of 4

© 2020 by Brian Alan Bild

ISBN: 978-1-63110-504-3

All Rights Reserved Under
International and Pan-American Copyright Conventions.
No part of this book may be used or reproduced in any manner whatsoever without written permission except in the case of brief quotations embodied in critical articles or reviews.

Women on cover art from left to right:
Maya Angelou, Nancy Pelosi, Emily Dickinson, Toni Morrison, Dolley Madison, Queen Elizabeth I, Rosa Parks, Jane Austen

Printed in the United States of America by
Graphic Connections Publishing
Chesterfield, Missouri 63005

Book 2 of 4

TABLE OF CONTENTS[1]

1996

1. Rock and Roll Beat 1
2. The Teacher Said 3

1997

3. The Rose Parade 4
4. The Great Big, Out of State, Octopus Bank ✔[2] 6
5. Ode to the Internet 8
6. One Dimension Less 9
7. The Easter Bunny ✔ 10
8. The Historic Yes Man 11
9. Cutting Up the Clock 13
10. The Obscure Thinker ✔ 14
11. Lilacs Down the Country Lane ✔ 16
12. English Poets 18
13. Machiavelli's Monster ✔ 19
14. I Don't Know ✔ 22

2001

15. Never a Word was Spoken ✔ 23

---

[1] The tables of contents for future Books Three and Four are also listed for future reference.

[2] Check marks (✔) signify special poems.

2005

16. American Sisyphus ✔ 24

2006

17. Precious Babies ✔ .27
18. Fools March Onward 29
19. An Ode to Female Legs ✔ 31
20. Love, a Lifetime Puzzle ✔ 33

2007

21. Listen 35
22. Sherman the Shetland Sheep Dog ✔ 37
23. I Cry ✔ 39
24. Why Say No? 41

2009

25. Mighty General Motors ✔ 43
26. Mandarin to Mandarin ✔ 45
27. A Daring Biker ✔ .47
28. The Great God Gimmie Stuff ✔ 48
29. A Battered Bugle .50
30. Changes 52

2010

31. My Pony ✔ 55

32.	Spring Flowers.	.56
33.	Wilted Flowers ✔	.57
34.	Nothing Bad Happens to BP (British Petroleum) ✔	.58
35.	The Beat ✔	.61
36.	The Seeker ✔	.63

2011

37.	The Gift	.65
38.	The Mighty Mississippi	.66
39.	The Wine of Life ✔	.67
40.	Love Ain't No Bait and Switch. ✔	.69
41.	Plato, Where Are You? (c) ✔	.72
42.	May Sunsets Last Forever ✔	.74
43.	Bertha, the Sweetest Rottweiler ✔	.76
44.	Barbara to Sandy: A Man's Lament for Shoes that Did Not Fit ✔	.77
45.	China's Vision	.80
46.	Monastery Garden ✔	.81
47.	River Waves (c)	.82
48.	Mother's Smile ✔	.83
49.	Onward Drove the 500 (c).	.84
50.	My Neighbor's Dogs	.86
51.	L.A. Freeway 2011	.87
52.	What's the Thing? (c)	.89
53.	Into the Fire of September 11, 2001 (c) ✔	.91
54.	Ding Dong Doggie	.93
55.	Strange Is the Land I Visit and See (c) ✔	.95

56. Christmas Time ✔ .96
57. An Unspoken Courthouse Creed (c) ✔ 97

2012

58. Love at a Distance ✔ 98
59. 99 to 1 99
60. Rain, Some Sun 102
61. Fetch, Floyd, Fetch! ✔ 104
62. Leading Onward ✔ 106
63. Politics as Poetry ✔ 108
64. Storms Ahead 111
65. Gypsy Moods ✔ 113
66. Spineless Little Worms 115
67. Lovely Illusions 117
68. When Horses Run Wild ✔ 118
69. Crotch Rocket 120
70. The Love of Mom and Dad 121
71. Baby Blue Eyes (c) ✔ 122
72. Mind Over Mouth (c) 123
73. Candy Wrappers (c) ✔ 124
74. Sea of Waves 126

2013

75. The Tunnel (c) ✔ 128
76. Droning On and On (c) ✔ 129
77. Carry the Candle 132
78. My Road Less Traveled (c) 133

Book 3 of 4

TABLE OF CONTENTS

2013

1. What Kind of Pigeons are in a Pigeon-Holed Brain
2. Big-Eyed Penny
3. I Am Mars
4. Little Princess Leia
5. American Assassins
6. Maple Tree
7. When I Gaze Upon Your Face
8. The Good and the Great
9. Change?
10. Thankfulness
11. Plato's Cave
12. Visit The Museum (c)
13. An Ode to Indigestion
14. Propolya Procession (c)
15. I am Not a Philosopher King (c)

2014

16. Chicken Noodle Soup
17. Life In Pictures
18. Brain Fart
19. Rover
20. Monet's Garden

21. "Convergence"
22. A Kind Hearted Gift
23. Bunnyland
24. Post Modern Lament
25. What's Missing?
26. Sequoias Are
27. Double Down, Double Down
28. Victory
29. Sand Castles?
30. Gazing Out the Window
31. Leading From Behind
32. I Miss "My" Floyd

2015

33. On My Veranda
34. Too Much Spilled Blood
35. So Many Tourists
36. Dressed Up Monkeys
37. No Dogs, Thank You
38. Changes in Life
39. The Ferguson Story has a Moral
40. The Wounding of Stare Decisis
41. When Daddy's Rich
42. A Thing of Beauty
43. A Cry from the Trenches
44. Dark Forces on the Move
45. A Tattoo can be Forever

46. America, the Land of Hype
47. Scrambled Eggs
48. Life is a Beach
49. Call Me Mars (c)
50. I Hear a Melody (c)
51. Assumptions and Conclusions
52. Tap Dance
53. Quiet Love (c)
54. Be Prepared

2016

55. The Devil's Balcony
56. Professors, Judges, Lawyers
57. My Toy Soldiers
58. Hyacinths
59. Sweet Lunacy
60. Bird Song (c)
61. The Alpha Dog Calls
62. Seattle Sardine (Flight 158)
63. Athletic Prowess (c)
64. Two Texas Cowboys
65. The Importance of Rhyme
66. Imaginary Animals
67. The Grim and Gritty Business of War
68. Poem For Amy and Friends..
69. America's Perfume
70. My Toes Speak in Couplets

71. Angels In Black? Doctors In Black?
72. Eureka!
73. Phalaenopsis
74. Rash Thoughts
75. My Stuffed Animals
76. Do You Remember?
77. The Day Kennedy Died
78. Thoughts After Midnight
79. Why Rhyme?
80. Electrified (c)
81. Beautiful Eyeful
82. Thoughtful Fantasy
83. Timely and Untimely Musings (c)
84. Ideology

Book 4 of 4

TABLE OF CONTENTS

2017

1. The Beach at Wakiki (c) . . . .
2. Who Is The Man? (c) . . . .
3. Independence of Mind . . . .
4. Keep Rolling Along . . . .
5. If I Were a Rich So and So . . . .
6. America is so Beautiful (c) . . . .
7. Call of the Alpha Dog . . . .
8. I Wonder . . . .
9. Words . . . .
10. Journeys . . . .
11. Trumpmud . . . .
12. The Dogs of War . . . .
13. Variations in Love . . . .
14. Many Perspectives (c) . . . .
15. Are Americans Fated to F _ _ _ Up? . . . .
16. Hurricane Winds and Hurricane Floods . . . .
17. In a Nutshell (It's the Economy Stupid or Hillary's Disease Becomes America's Disease) . . . .
18. Count the Full Cost (c) . . . .
19. When I Go Shopping . . . .
20. On the Planet Donald . . . .
21. I Say to Myself "Why Change?" . . . .

22. Old Plaster, New Plaster . . . .
23. The Tiger Stalks His Prey (c) . . . .
24. Gun Power (P-O-W-E-R) . . . .
25. The European Question . . . .
26. Why Can't All the World, Think Like Me? . . . .
27. America is Bleeding . . . .
28. The Oak and the Maple (c) . . . .
29. Loving Too Much . . . .
30. My Machine Gun . . . .
31. Hitchhikers, Hijackers, Vampires, Hurricanes. . . . .

2018

32. Wartime Soldiering . . . .
33. Stand Pat and the Landlord (A Tale of Two T _ _ds) . . . .
34. The River Flows . . . .
35. Government for the Greedy . . . .
36. Reconciliation . . . .
37. Twenty-Sixteen was a Fashionable Year . . . .
38. Our Principled President . . . .
39. Rainbow Maker . . . .
40. Kindness and Generosity . . . .
41. The Pied Piper of Hollow Propaganda . . . .
42. One Player is Silent . . . .
43. My Jalopy . . . .
44. America Creates Great Poverty . . . .
45. Chasing Skirts, Pursuing Trousers (c). . . . .
46. A Serious Rhyming Poem, About Birth Control Pills . . .

47. The First Casualty of War . . . .
48. Different Optics . . . .
49. The Shame of Men in Power . . . .
50. Convoluted Logic . . . .
51. Lifetime Journeys . . . .
52. The Scenic Sewers of Cerberus . . . .
53. Again, What is Beauty? (c) . . . .
54. Paintings and Frames . . . .
55. A More Rounded Humanity . . . .

2019

56. Shall We Dance . . . .
57. Oh What A Beautiful Nose . . . .
58. Trump's Jalopy Joyride into Yesterday . . . .
59. Bittersweet Time . . . .
60. Donald's Delirium . . . .
61. Why the Silence? . . . .
62. The Amazing Rolodex Scholar . . . .
63. America and Nirvana . . . .
64. Percy Dovertonsils Revisited (c) . . . .
65. Paradise (c) . . . .
66. My Mister Wonderful (c) . . . .
67. Norway's Beauty . . . .

2020

68. Starry Night . . . .
69. Donald's Award . . . .

– xiii –

70. My Dog Mo . . . .
71. Are We Family (fam-i-ly) . . . .
72. Imagination and Early Success . . . .
73. The Airplane Known as Fubar . . . .
74. The White House is Haunted . . . .
75. Donald Trump, the Master Chef . . . .
76. Turning the Corner . . . .
77. The White House as Circus Tent . . . .
78. Ice Cream Girl. . . . .

ROCK AND ROLL BEAT

by

Brian Alan Bild

© 1996

Listen, can you hear it?
Have you heard the news?
Again, better than ever,
Get out your rock and roll shoes!

Bill Haley and the Comets,
Boy, could they rock.
On and on, they would,
Rock around the clock.

Chuck Berry and others,
Gave a big start.
Many thanks to them,
For doing their part.

Elvis Presley leads the way,
Many others on his heels.
Love that rock and roll beat,
You know how it feels.

Chubby Checker,
Twist, twist, twist.
Back and forth,
Here in our midst.

Tina Turner,
She's dynamite.
Her high powered rock,
Beats through the night.

The beat, the beat,
Drives the music on.
Dance to the beat,
Of a rock and roll song.

THE TEACHER SAID

by

Brian Alan Bild

© 1996

It's obvious! It's obvious!
So the teacher said:
How could anything else,
Be inside your head?

Obviously important,
It means the world to me.
You must understand.
Why can't you see?

My surprise to you.
Guess by what I've said.
You must heed my word,
And know what's in my head.

THE ROSE PARADE

by

Brian Alan Bild

© 1997

A visual delight,
The Rose Parade.
Pictures and floats,
In flowers made.

For years and years,
But once a year.
The flower pageant,
Of scenes most dear.

In three dimensions,
Moving in a row,
The flower pictures,
Beam and glow.

Around the world,
We gaze at flowers.
Their style and grace,
On floats self-powered.

Visions of flowers,
And a bright, sunny day.
Arise in the heart,
Each New Year's Day.

Contrived, unrealistic,
Artistic nonetheless.
Floral visions amaze,
Excite and bless.

Cascades of flowers,
Beguile and inspire.
A true hocus pocus,
Of artistic desires.

Called to Pasadena,
On visual alert.
Gorgeous flowers,
Arise from simple dirt.

Floral imagination,
In scenes so contrived.
A hypnotic spectacle,
You cannot deny.

Pharaohs, spaceships,
And circus clowns.
Childhood dreams,
Make the world go round.

THE GREAT BIG, OUT OF STATE, OCTOPUS BANK

by

Brian Alan Bild

© 1997

Look out! Here it comes!
Unstoppable as a tank.
The great Big, Out of State,
Octopus Bank.

Financial colossus,
They say of high rank.
That Great, Big, Out of State
Octopus Bank.

Monstrous, money-sucking,
Mammoth machine.
Horrible reality,
Nightmare of your dreams.

Money here, money there,
The bank consumes it all.
The huge financial monster,
Trumpets a mighty call.

Money-hungry bank,
Of appetite unceasing.
Behind the scenes force,
Of momentum increasing.

A monetary magnet,
Of incredible force.
After money, your money,
And also mine, of course.

Beware the power of greenbacks,
Stacked in a vault.
Acquiring all the money,
Is not the poor bank's fault.

Economics, economics,
They say it's thus and such.
The bank wants all the money,
That tentacles touch.

Somewhere in the building,
Bankers count their gain.
From the sweat of others,
And the worker's pain.

The Great BOO Bank,
Has tentacles of control,
That reach throughout the land,
And grab its very soul.

ODE TO THE INTERNET

by

Brian Alan Bild

© 1997

Electronic goddess,
Wisk me away.
You are my escape.
What can I say?

Amazing electronics,
My mind goes to play.
Inside bytes and pieces,
Games blow you away.

The flick of a switch,
And off I go.
Electronic maze,
Of thus and so.

ONE DIMENSION LESS

by

Brian Alan Bild

© 1997

Thinking little,
Active nonetheless.
A surface soul,
Is one dimension less.

I am the man,
With the surface soul.
Active in business,
With the heart of a troll.

Less than the heroes,
The men of old,
Who knew themselves,
And causes bold.

I worked hard,
Never knew a pun.
Was a good provider,
Didn't have much fun.

THE EASTER BUNNY

by

Brian Alan Bild

© 1997

I believe in the Easter Bunny,
Though my children don't.
Glory and celebration,
In spring, I do not doubt.

Hop, hop, hop away,
Into our daily lives.
The silly, spring bunny,
Tells us, spring's arrived.

THE HISTORIC YES MAN

by

Brian Alan Bild

© 1997

Some look high and low,
In places far and wide,
For an eternal "yes" man,
And thoughts that coincide.

Lackies in many colors,
Within this land of ours.
Many seek his "Yes, sir!"
To gaze upon the stars.

Black, white, brown or blue,
Lackies come in many hues.
To a lonely, tyrant,
Lackies pay their dues.

Nothing else pleases,
As simple, syllables such.
The crisp reply "Yes, sir!"
Are the lackies' magic touch.

Forever, forever, and forever,
I live through history.
The loyal "yes man" speaks,
My one eternal story.

(It) Could be getting along,
Some say politic.
But the "yes man" always,
Gets in his licks.

CUTTING UP THE CLOCK

by

Brian Alan Bild

© 1997

Time, time, time,
How to spend our time?
Cutting up the clock,
Is no simple rhyme.

Being in many places,
With many a clarion call.
Choices here, choices there,
How to do it all?

One way or another,
A choice for what is best.
The ways we spend our time,
Guides us to the rest.

The tasks, the time, the choices,
Our conscience lets us know.
The guiding, internal compass,
That lets our spirit grow.

THE OBSCURE THINKER

by

Brian Alan Bild

© 1997

The obscure thinker,
Spies one in a million.
The exception to the exception,
On a good day, one in a billion.

He doesn't know the ending,
Doesn't know where to begin.
Stacking so many angels,
On the head of a pin.

If this plus that,
Is divided by pi,
My convoluted reasoning,
Makes me a super guy.

The lesson is greater,
And so is this and such.
My thoughts are terrific,
I really know so much.

Needles in a haystack,
Are my specialty.
My strange preoccupation,
Needles set me free.

The more obscure the better,
With tangents, I'm sublime.
A riddle inside a puzzle,
Strange reasons, they are mine.

The Middle Ages, the Middle Ages,
Are just heaven to me.
My thoughts are with Aquinas,
I am truly he.

I'm lost in thought,
That lived long ago.
The obscure thinker,
Is backwards on the go.

LILACS DOWN THE COUNTRY LANE

by

Brian Alan Bild

© 1997

Picture in your mind,
A sunny, country lane,
An older English cottage,
For visits once again.

Along that lane in spring,
Are lilacs all around.
The lilac scent is everywhere,
The fragrance so abounds.

Nature's perfume,
Delights the senses so.
Lilacs truly are the best,
As down that lane you go.

Lilacs, potent lilacs,
Their fragrance a delight.
The perfume of angels,
As they grace the night.

Lilacs do distract,
Their compelling lilac scent.
Of nature's fragrant flowers,
Such aroma they present.

Lilacs down the country lane,
So bold, yet out of sight.
I love the smell, as you can tell,
Soul and body have delight.

But truly lilacs, you cannot know,
By paper, ink and words.
Go out and smell the lilacs,
Enjoy the great outdoors.

ENGLISH POETS

by

Brian Alan Bild

© 1997

Countless English poets,
Describe life, large and small.
Of monumental passions,
They wrote about it all.

Of mythical characters,
In strange, exotic places.
Of embarrassed pseudo-lovers,
With blush red, startled faces.

From Samarkan to Xanadu,
Foreign places still unknown.
Of broken hearts and loveless lives,
Throughout the world they've gone.

Penned lines, both long and short,
Some of this, and some of that.
By blending lines together,
Poems are not forgot.

MACHIAVELLI'S MONSTER

by

Brian Alan Bild

© 1997

Machiavelli's monster,
So the rumor and the talk.
Like an overgrown monster,
Of Jack 'n' the beanstalk.

The giant fumbles onward,
Crushing small things on his way.
The mammoth, predatory monster,
Stumbles through his days.

Fearing this government monster,
Like some headless horror.
Yet, his clumsy misdeeds,
We see in our mirror.

The governed scorn the government,
For presumed incompetence.
Strange partners in life,
Step to a stranger dance.

Government departments,
Attract our discontent.
Those salaried bureaucrats,
Personify mis-government.

On a grand scale,
We fear government,
Those misdirected agents,
The government has sent.

Our monsters of the night,
That roam the dark forest,
Are Machiavelli's monsters,
Our fears to the fullest?

Machiavelli's monsters,
Wild beasts of our day.
Inhabit a fearful forest,
At our work and play.

Many of our monsters,
Are in our minds alone.
Shaking up our thoughts,
Those monsters, never gone.

Desiring a revelation,
A change from daily life.
The land of OZ seems empty,
Cold and dark as night.

Grand visions escape us.
The fears are so compelling.
Routine sustains us,
In cave-like dwellings.

Machiavelli's monsters,
We see them everywhere.
Knowing no boundaries,
Our fears are here and there.

Does Machiavelli's monster,
Have a conscience or a soul,
Can government assist us,
When we hate, and fear it so?

Can it tear you apart,
Without compassion or remorse?
Greatly out of control,
A vast, unstoppable force.

Are we mental pygmies,
Struggling up to our ears?
Casting unto others,
The shortcomings of our fears.

Our leaders lack vision,
Because we lack it too.
A myopic perspective,
Won't reveal much that's new.

I DON'T KNOW

by

Brian Alan Bild

© 1997

Don't know what "I love you." means,
I guess I never will.
Whenever we're together,
You give my heart a thrill.

The new ways to love you,
Excite me – and always will.
A new way to say "I love you,"
My heart just won't stay still.

To the future times,
We spend together – us,
Forever and forever,
I'll always say, "God bless."

NEVER A WORD WAS SPOKEN

by

Brian Alan Bild

© 2001

Charming, truly charming,
She's a beauty to watch.
A warm expressive face,
Fetching torso to match.

Round full cheeks,
Accompany her smile.
Bright, happy eyes,
Dazzle and beguile.

Hips not too large,
Longer legs to match.
A wonderful figure,
Such a glorious catch.

Enjoy your springtime looks,
Your vibrancy, your life,
Life is ever changing,
For such a pretty wife.

AMERICAN SISYPHUS[1]

by

Brian Alan Bild

© 2005

Cookie cutter people
In cookie cutter stores
March, march, they enter
Through cookie cutter doors.
Wringing every penny
From the penny jar,
Hypnotized by low price,
Their dollars don't go far.

Trapped by low wages,
And rising living costs.
"Free" trade keeps wages low,
Inflation hurts the most.
Free trade! Free trade!
Economic battle cry,
Wages stay so low,
We can't afford to buy.

---

[1] In Greek mythology, Sisyphus was cursed by a never-ending task. He would roll a large stone up a hill. Each time as he approached the top, the stone slipped to the bottom and he has to begin all over again.

No union to protect us
Our wages they stay flat.
The rising tide of prices
May drown us just like that.
The daily money struggle,
Nickels, dimes and pennies.
Will the dollars stretch?
Will we be left with any?

The Almighty Dollar
No matter what the rate.
With cards stacked against us,
A money-grabbing fate.
Culture, enjoyment
Leisure times and such,
Gone from daily life,
They cost too much.

Some drive BMW's
Some drive tiny cars.
Downhill the country's going,
No matter who you are.
Give up, give up,
When will Americans give up?
When effort makes no sense,
America will give up.

The force is against us,
The dollars are so few,
Always chasing dollars,
Turns a person blue.
The economic pundits
Deaf and dumb they are,
Silence is golden
For economic stars.

The economic headlights,
Are looking pretty dim.
Helpless in a sea of debt
How can a person win?
Generations in the future,
Are burdened with our debt,
Our legacy of debt
Where is their safety net?

Misspent funds are,
Fiscal pollution.
Our short term greed,
Needs a military solution!
The iron bars, the bars
Of economic prison.
Made of dollar signs,
For political reasons.

PRECIOUS BABIES

by

Brian Alan Bild

© 2006

Silent sentry to the future,
Is every babe in arms.
Watchful, caring parents,
Keep them safe, from winter storms.

Jolly, rolly pollies,
Smile bright as any sun.
Gifts of God from heaven,
Pure joy to dad and mum.

Oh, joyous days for babies,
Precious gifts to the earth.
How wonderful and joyous,
Days of happiness and mirth.

Cherished, small and wonderful,
Those windows of the future.
The best of life to all,
May all the world nurture.

Chubby little babies,
Source of innocent fun.
What, oh what will happen,
In decades yet to come?

FOOLS MARCH ONWARD

by

Brian Alan Bild

© 2006

The chain of fools continues,
As if it has no end.
Bound by apparitions,
That they hold and defend.

One fool after another,
Blindly dances round.
Around and around and around,
Where nothing new is found.

Repeating their apparitions,
In a gobbledygook of sound.
Looking for their conscience,
They have never found.

Always in lockstep,
The leaders do require.
No room for departure,
From apparitions' desire.

Reality has no meaning,
For this chain of fools.
Two nations hemorrhage,
Immersed in bloody pools.

Doubly red, in ink and blood,
The spiral leads down and down.
Is there a national conscience?
Somehow, to be found?

Unlike those famous blind men,
We can open our eyes,
Seeing the elephant clearly
What if the elephant dies?

AN ODE TO FEMALE LEGS

by

Brian Alan Bild

© 2006

Venus wants her arms,
But I'll take the legs,
The gorgeous smooth taper
For them I'd plead and beg.

The roundness, the curves,
The proportions so fine
I adore them, I do.
They're mine, mine, mine.

Showgirl legs are,
Artistry in motion.
The canter, the sway,
My heart's great devotion.

The excitement, the beauty
Those long, lean curves,
Back and forth, back and forth,
A calming rhythm for the nerves.

Legs can say it all,
In oh, so many ways.
So lovely to look at
To brighten the days.

Time and time again,
The fascinating beauty,
Men looked and looked,
Such was their duty.

Mesmerized by beauty,
As hormones clarify.
For time and time again
Men wonder as they sigh.

Sometimes they're running
Sometimes they dance.
The wonder of movement
Adds to the romance.

Look and appreciate
Those long, lean lines.
A little bit of heaven
A dash of the divine.

LOVE, A LIFETIME PUZZLE

by

Brian Alan Bild

© 2006

Love, a lifetime puzzle,
How will the pieces fit?
Rearranging our lives,
Slowly, bit by bit.

Looking back upon the years,
I think of days gone by,
Of what I did and didn't do,
My thoughts are drawing neigh.

When love was young and blessed,
In all its ways and forms,
Love in all its purity,
Without routine or norms.

Wonder of wonders,
Love so young and free,
Changing to rediscover,
What love was meant to be.

Changing and rearranging,
Our thoughts and our lives,
Life is love displayed,
Within hellos and goodbyes.

Seemingly strange and confused,
For young love to change.
Other times, love's misused,
Love's power to rearrange.

Where will the power take you,
Up to the clouds above,
Or down into the depths?
Such is the power of love.

The dimensions of love,
Vast and multicolored,
Dwelling in each life,
Comprehensive as no other.

LISTEN

by

Brian Alan Bild

© 2007

Listen. Listen.
What can it be?
Angelic voices,
Harken to me.

A chorus, a choir,
Ephemeral sounds.
Joy of the heavens,
On earth it resounds.

Over and over,
Through hills and plains,
The glories of heaven,
Momentarily remain.

Like none other,
Sounds float in the air,
As comfort and joy,
For listeners who care.

Spiritual blessings,
Those unseen sounds,
Float in the air,
Completely surround.

Yes, the sounds end,
Still silence remains.
'Twas a moment apart,
Those joyful refrains.

Out of nothing,
The glorious strains.
All quiet now,
The songs come again.

SHERMAN THE SHETLAND SHEEP DOG[1]

by

Brian Alan Bild

© 2007

Sherman the Shetland sheep dog,
Playful as a dog can be,
Always alert and helpful,
You are such a dog for me.

One day, as I was walking,
Saw a Sheltie mother dog,
She and her baby wandering,
Lost, and looking all agog.

I approached the doggies,
Hesitant they backed away.
Nearby was auto traffic,
That's no place for doggie play.

Fearful of the autos,
I followed them all around.
They did avoid the traffic,
Just one doggie to be found.

---

[1] Recite to the tune "Rudolph the Red Nose Reindeer"

Strange way to find a doggie,
I love him just the same,
My wonderful companion,
Little Sherman is his name.

I CRY

by

Brian Alan Bild

© 2007

The Statue of Liberty
Stepped down one day,
Wiping away her tears,
As she began to pray.

I cry for America,
Going the wrong way,
A country leading backward,
Alive in yesterday.

I cry for America,
And you would too.
Great things are happening,
But our accomplishments are few.

I cry for America,
Once mighty and great,
Wandering around in circles,
Lost as she debates.

I cry for America.
What shall we do?
Live our lives head on,
Believing we can do.

I cry for America.
Shall we lead somewhere?
The future lies before us,
For us to do and care.

WHY SAY NO?

by

Brian Alan Bild

© 2007

Shall we occupy Iraq?
It's a walk in the park.
Yet, blood and death claim every day.
Ignoring the chaos, I hit the mark.

This war's not costing very much,
Three trillion dollars or more,
No better way to spend it.
We're just evening the score.

Healthcare's such a luxury.
We'll all die anyway.
The poor don't need such luxuries.
Religion carries their day.

Medicare is going broke.
Who cares? Really, not I.
The Democrats created it.
To Republicans, pie in the sky.

I don't care about CO2.
Unseen, it doesn't exist.
It's not hurting anyone,
Complaining should cease and desist.

Halliburton wants contracts,
Large, lucrative as can be.
Mountains of greenbacks everywhere,
Their profits will make us free.

Call me your loyal president.
I have no mind of my own.
No way could I care less about you,
I'm a Republican clone.

MIGHTY GENERAL MOTORS

by

Brian Alan Bild

© 2009

Amongst the dusty files,
In New York Bankruptcy Court,
There lives a tale of greed,
And capitalism <u>de</u> <u>mort</u>.

For decade after decade,
Cadillac, Buick, Corvette,
A cavalcade of excellence,
GM cars were best.

Mighty General Motors,
Colossus of the West.
In the 20th Century,
Better than the rest.

Committees are correct,
In every way they can.
Salvation by committee,
That's where GM stands.

For decades GM stood,
The richest of the rich.
GM can make just anything,
Car buyers will not switch.

Don't make the best of cars,
Skimp yearly to get by.
GM wants profits,
Great cars go bye, bye.

Concentrating on profit,
Those profits came to an end.
You don't need a good car,
Trust GM, "I'm your friend."

Imports, they don't matter,
So said the mighty GM.
Americans are loyal to,
Whatever's built for them.

Japanese engineers,
Aiming for the stars,
Yearly they perfected,
The most reliable of cars.

So goes the chase for greenbacks,
A mindless story of sorts.
Mighty General Motors,
Died in New York City Bankruptcy Court.

MANDARIN TO MANDARIN

by

Brian Alan Bild

© 2009

In Ancient China one day,
One mandarin said to another.
(Since we talk only to each other.)
Ignore all those others.
They're not our brothers.
Thinking they'll try,
But never get by,
Such are the rules of heaven.

"What shall we think about today?"
Thoughts so obscure
No doubt will endure.
A mandarin's fate
To regurgitate,
So many a date
And not differentiate,
What was heard so long ago.

Paid for our moldy, half loaf,
Minds sharpened to a point.
Must not disappoint.
There's nothing to it.
How would ancients do it?
Being totally advanced
Our minds are enhanced,
Thinking great thoughts each day.

They dare not criticize,
If they do not realize,
What the hell we are doing.

A DARING BIKER

by

Brian Alan Bild

© 2009

One day he rode away
A daring biker he.
Nothing stopped him.
Bold as brass was he.

Weaving through daily traffic
Just between you and me.
Fearless of physics and mass,
His speed would set him free.

What good are safety devices
When speed makes you be?
Such a biker! What a biker!
Can't you see, can't he see?

One day he didn't come back,
One day he didn't come back.

THE GREAT GOD GIMMIE STUFF

by

Brian Alan Bild

© 2009

The Great God Gimmie Stuff,
Walks across the land.
He wanders everywhere,
With an outstretched hand.

Gimmie this, gimmie that,
Don't care what it is.
I'll acquire all the stuff,
Be it yours, hers or his.

Gimmie this, gimmie that,
Gimmie, gimmie, gimmie,
Yes, I want everything,
Even Mickey's Minnie.

I've never enough, never,
That's one thing for sure.
Stuff, stuff, I collect stuff.
For greed there is no cure.

Don't know what to do with stuff
I have so much of it.
I can't have everything,
I'll surely throw a fit.

More, more, always more,
I don't know when to quit.
I want all, yes everything
I want every little bit.

Alas, there'll come a day
When I make no noise.
They'll dig one enormous pit
And bury me, with my toys.

A BATTERED BUGLE

by

Brian Alan Bild

© 2009

As I walked among the tulips,
On a breezy, pleasant day,
I spied a forlorn bugle,
Greatly battered; wouldn't play.

Dust and dirt surrounded,
Where the battered bugle lay,
Beside the beaten path,
On that breezy, pleasant day.

In my imagination,
What could that bugle be?
An instrument for concerts
With musical memories?

Or could there have been,
Another bugle call?
The sound of marching men,
Brings down a Jericho Wall?

Could there have been,
A different bugle call?
The sound of wounds and death,
The sound of those who fall.

Justice through war,
Inspires the souls of men.
If, war is just,
War must seek an end.

The whirlwinds of war
Encourage those at home.
With thousands dying,
When will this be done?

Violence, more violence
In visions from afar.
Does bloodlust addiction,
Continue violence and war?

Why should people die?
Reality disappoints.
Lost causes do not prosper,
Though the departed, we anoint.

CHANGES

by

Brian Alan Bild

© 2009

Just finished high school,
With arms of steel.
Quickly got a job,
Making what's real.

Paid real well,
For making those things.
Loved that job,
And the cash box ring.

My job and I,
We both did fine.
Did my part,
For heavenly design.

My job, my job,
Routine it may be.
Good pay for anything,
That's the job for me.

Had a great car,
And a wife to boot.
Had three kids,
And a Sunday suit.

Cruising right along,
My car, my wife.
Everything in synch,
A wonderful life.

Decade after decade,
Cruising right along.
Life so happy,
Singing my song.

Small cog in the wheel,
How did it feel?
Didn't matter,
My life was real.

Floating just floating.
The family canoe.
Pleasant situation,
For all I knew.

Decade after decade,
Inflation sucked me in.
Tighter and tighter,
My head in a spin.

Slowly life is tight.
Hard to butter bread.
Wage stagnation,
So the TV said.

As the years go by,
I feel like a boy.
My life's not right.
A rich man's toy?

Blame myself,
Or just get mad?
Don't know what to think,
'Bout a life turned bad.

Angered, disgusted,
My life shouldn't be,
Struggle in America,
Land of the free.

Topsy, turvey,
Such is life.
Land of abundance,
A land of strife.

MY PONY

by

Brian Alan Bild

© 2010

My dad was a pony,
Many years ago,
When I was in diapers,
A tiny thus and so.

He'd crawl upon the floor,
I'd be on his back.
Sister held his bridle,
We all got in the act.

Happy times together,
Many years ago.
Pretending, pretending,
A world of our own.

SPRING FLOWERS

by

Brian Alan Bild

© 2010

Throughout the days and nights,
For years and seasons long
Let us raise our voices
And sing a happy song.

New flowers and green grass,
Once again, spring is here,
Tulips and daffodils
So dear and now, so near.

Look beyond, look beyond,
Harvest expectation,
The warmth and joy of life
Hope of repetition.

WILTED FLOWERS

by

Brian Alan Bild

© 2010

From the mighty redwoods,
To the smallest flowers.
There will come a time,
For the last of hours.

Each life is not forever,
Though we wish it so.
The finest of flowers,
Will not their glories show.

Enjoy tomorrow's flowers,
Remember flowers past.
For even the flowers
They do not everlast.

NOTHING BAD HAPPENS TO BP (BRITISH PETROLEUM)

by

Brian Alan Bild

© 2010

    In our business there's no referee.
    Big and bold are we.
    Rules? What rules? Not for me.
    We do what we want and shout with glee.
Seems, nothing bad happens to BP.

    Some things we don't take seriously.
    Kings of the world, that's who we be.
    Just think of us a mad bumble bee.
    We act as we please with impunity.
Seems, nothing bad happens to BP.

    We bubble and babble incoherently,
    Lie out our teeth perniciously.
    We look at disaster dispassionately.
    Shall we rest? It's time for tea.
Seems, nothing bad happens to BP.

In search of profits, polluting the sea,
Monstrously large, can't you see.
My what a mess, how could it be?
The mess is your problem, yes siree.
Seems, nothing bad happens to BP.

Modern day piracy out on the sea.
Damaging others means nothing to me.
Despite requests and many a plea,
We mumble and fumble to a great degree.
Seems, nothing bad happens to BP.

Wind pushes the oil, there is no lee.
Multitudes of creatures cease to be.
Justice? Will justice never be?
BP dollars are all we see.
Seems, nothing bad happens to BP.

America suffers? We see no misery.
Promise anything facetiously.
Yes, our monster from under the sea.
Fear not, we wouldn't hurt a flea.
Seems, nothing bad happens to BP.

Out oil flows mercilessly.
Clean up costs billions. The pollution is free.
Free, free the pollution is free.
All is sugar coated even our tea.
Seems, nothing bad happens to BP.

Death and destruction wherever it be.
To hell with safety, its dollars we see.
A fountain of oil under the sea.
We see no responsibility.
Seems, nothing bad happens to BP.

There's no mess, just opportunity.
That's why we act relunctantly.

THE BEAT

by

Brian Alan Bild

© 2010

Hear it from housetops?
Can't keep my seat,
Once I hear the beat
Way down the street.
Got the beat, beat, beat,
In my feet, feet, feet.

They say indiscrete,
Nor is it unique.
There's no defeating,
A musical treat.
Got the beat, beat, beat,
In my feet, feet, feet.

When the beat comes down,
Like a wave of heat,
With a driving beat,
There is no retreat.
Got the beat, beat, beat,
In my feet, feet, feet.

With no driving beat,
Life's so incomplete.
Can you hear the beat?
Let's repeat the beat.
Got the beat, beat, beat.
In my feet, feet, feet.

THE SEEKER[1]

by

Brian Alan Bild

© 2010

I love sweet money,
How much have you got?
Maybe it's millions,
Maybe it's not.

I love the crinkle of greenbacks, so green,
My love of money, of money I dream.
I love sweet money,
For me and my team.

My favorite diamonds
Are big all around.
I do love diamonds
They're safe and they're sound.

Diamonds glitter, as nothing I know,
Wonderful diamonds.
A bright, shiny glow
My favorite diamonds.

---

[1] To the tune of "How Deep is the Ocean"

Gold through my fingers,
The thrill of pure gold.
I'm so in heaven
When gold I can hold.

If you could see it,
My heart is pure gold.
Gold does bedazzle,
On gold I am sold.
Gold through my fingers
The thrill of pure gold.

THE GIFT

by

Brian Alan Bild

© 2011

I have not roses,
My love, as a sign.
I lay at your feet,
This heart of mine.

THE MIGHTY MISSISSIPPI

by

Brian Alan Bild

© 2011

The mighty Mississippi
Rolls on, and on, and on,
The never-ending river
Every sunset to dawn.

Never-ending nourishment
For soybeans, wheat and corn.
Soil, light and rain combine
The food for life is born.

Quiet sustainer of life
For multiple millions.
All placed around the globe
Russians to Brazilians.

The mighty Mississippi,
Force of nature and life
Feeding the hungry millions
Bringing the world delight.

THE WINE OF LIFE

by

Brian Alan Bild

© 2011

The taste and sparkle,
Make wine so fine.
These blended joys,
Are liquid sunshine.

Such taste and sparkle,
Combine together.
Exquisitely blended,
Complement each other.

As if by angels,
To a realm divine.
The blending we share,
It's yours and mine.

The blend of forever
With the here and now
A blessed combination
An unavoidable "wow".

It's something so special,
A nourishment sublime.
The magic of blending,
Is hard to define.

A toast to blended love,
Here's to us, we two.
When wine is a symbol,
Even water will do.

The taste and sparkle,
So need each other.
If exquisitely blended,
They're lasting lovers.

Naturally, yet unnaturally,
To another realm, divine.
Joy and comfort continually
Swept away, be mine, be mine.

The taste and sparkle,
Make wine so fine.
As blended joys,
They magically shine.

LOVE AIN'T NO BAIT AND SWITCH

by

Brian Alan Bild

©2011

Sometime's I stop,
To look across the years.
Sometimes I'm happy,
Other times, in tears.

I've met many a woman,
Over life's course.
Some for the better,
Some for the worse.

Females can be illusions,
Not being as they seem.
Others are constant,
Much more than a dream.

The truest love is constant,
Not hither and yon.
Always with you,
Whatever you've done.

If you are lucky,
It started with mom.
The blessed person,
From whom you've come.

Though a helpless baby,
Or child growing up,
No matter your course,
As a frisky little pup.

She and others like her,
Were there by your side.
Spirit of togetherness,
None would divide.

That steady spirit,
Is your lifelong friend.
The spirit's there,
No matter your end.

Luckier still,
Is a man with a wife.
Another companion,
To journey through life.

That steady spirit,
With its love so fine,
Warms the heart,
Yours and mine.

Loving spirits,
In tune with each other.
Spiritual parents,
Spiritual others.

These loving spirits,
Don't bait and switch.
Always there,
No spiritual kitsch.

Sort through the kitsch,
Find what is best.
Keep the loving spirits,
They're not like the rest.

PLATO, WHERE ARE YOU? (c)

by

Brian Alan Bild

© 2011

Plato where are you?
Remembered by so few.
Dead on your pages,
Nurtured Dark Ages.

Do you survive?
Do you thrive?
Answers where are you?
Are they among the few?

Do abstracts matter?
Do we just get fatter?
With food, clothing, plumbing,
Do we know what's coming?

What's the best of life?
Three squares; a lack of strife?
Religion gives some solace.
Abstracts give us balance.

Is there any elation,
About civilization?
Abstract thought it be,
Joy for all to "see."

What is justice?
Where is happiness?
They cannot be seen.
Where have they been?

What is real reality?
What can it be?
Can we see it,
When we think a bit?

Am I lost in a cave,
Like a silly knave?
Do I know the riddle,
Or do I simply twiddle (my thumbs)?

MAY SUNSETS LAST FOREVER

by

Brian Alan Bild

© 2011

Oh, the Greeks of old,
Loved to look and say:
A rosy-fingered dawn
Brings the light of day.

Almost in forgetfulness,
The Greeks ignored the sky,
When the day was over,
And night was drawing nigh.

Few words they spoke of sunsets.
Were they hidden in plain sight?
Clouds in combinations,
Bathed in pastel light.

As if angel kisses,
Spread across the sky.
Sunsets paint their pictures,
As centuries slide by.

Painters have not mastered,
Nature's kaleidoscope.
The glories of the skies,
Warm, like love and hope.

Fleeting vivid colors,
Before the time of sleep.
Illusive summer sunsets,
I'd like to catch and keep.

BERTHA, THE SWEETEST ROTTWEILER

by

Brian Alan Bild

©2011

It was sad, Big "bad" Bertha died,
The sweetest dog you'd ever meet.
Tender to people and all dogs.
Gentle Rottweiler, that's a feat.

She was a faithful companion,
Docile, canine mother spirit.
Beautiful tan and black markings,
With gentility she wore it.

Although she knew few doggie tricks,
Her fetching was full of vigor,
Quiet, muscular, well-behaved,
Not a barker, not a digger.

Remember her peaceful presence,
She so enjoyed attention.
Like all the living; her time had come,
Not so curious, now contented.

BARBARA TO SANDY:
A MAN'S LAMENT
FOR SHOES THAT DID NOT FIT

by

Brian Alan Bild

© 2011

Yes, Barbara.[1]
Beautiful face,
Just one look, could,
Make your heart race.

Betty, Betty,
Soft and pretty,
Such a vision,
In the city.

Jane, oh yes, Jane,
With curves so round.
Her skin so soft,
Rightfully proud.

Judy, Judy,
A goddess figure.
The way she walks,
Is <u>de rigor.</u>

---

[1] The fictitious females are named in alphabetical order.

She was my Kay,
Could make my day.
Fun is serious,
Fun is play.

Kathy, my friend.
Smart as a whip.
Fast as lightening
Lips with a quip.

Mary, Mary,
Not contrary.
Fun, yes fun,
I dare not tary.

Maureen, Maureen,
Bit of a snob.
Tender is the heart
She just might rob.

Oh, Pamela,
Sings like a bird
That sweetest sound,
I've ever heard.

My Patricia
Woman so fine
Fabled kisses,
Like sweet wine.

Oh my, Peggy,
Peggy, Peggy
Her affections,
Were so ready.

My Rose, my Rose.
Finest flower,
Of the garden
For us, it's our(s).

Ruth's a beauty,
Peaches and cream.
Quiet and kind,
Wonderful dream.

Sandy, Sandy,
Ponytail girl.
She turns her head,
Pony tail whirls.

CHINA'S VISION

by

Brian Alan Bild

© 2011

China looks forward,
Glimpsing better days.
As the farmer sees,
And the scholar says.

China reawakens,
Seeing sunny days,
Blending new with old,
There's greatness in her ways.

Modern and prosperous,
So her future seems.
Referring to her past,
China dreams, great dreams.

MONASTERY GARDEN

by

Brian Alan Bild

© 2011

In a monastery garden,
Tranquility waits for me.
Courtyard of contemplation,
Quietness, you do not see.

In the calm delights of nature,
Quiet restfulness is the goal.
Peacefulness for the spirit,
Restores a tired soul.

In a monastery garden,
Where time and worry depart.
The mind is opened and cleansed.
Mental renewal, becomes art.

RIVER WAVES (c)

by

Brian Alan Bild

© 2011

Waves on the river, roll on and on,
Whatever, the weather, roll on and on.

Gentle waves roll, and lap the shore.
The river and life flow evermore.

Both joy and force of nature's earth,
The water and waves, give life rebirth.

Forward, so forward the river flows,
Steadily onward, on it goes.

The lovely life of a flowing river,
Where nature and life combine forever.

MOTHER'S SMILE

by

Brian Alan Bild

© 2011

The sweetness of a mother's smile,
Warms the home and all within.
Her joy and kindness, please the soul,
With her love for kith and kin.

ONWARD DROVE THE 500 (c)

by

Brian Alan Bild

© 2011

Seems rather silly,
To race willy-nilly.
For 500 miles
And millions of smiles.

I do love fast cars,
But it seems bizarre.
Such a long race,
At such a fast pace.

Millions for a race car,
Win or lose they are.
Thousands take their seats,
Millions in gate receipts.

Thirty-three times millions,
Is dollars in gazillions.
The race games go on,
So one car can win.

If you race for (2 ½) hours,
Receive a wreath of flowers,
You win by just a wink,
What do people think?

Number two has lost,
By seconds the cost.
Such an inferior car,
Its record does mar.

The spur of competition,
Is the holy mission.
To win, to win,
That's the state we're in.

MY NEIGHBORS' DOGS

by

Brian Alan Bild

© 2011

Lolly and Lilly,
A happy crew.
Wonderful companions,
That's what they do.

Yorkies are playmates,
Wide-eyed and furry.
With quizzical looks,
They have no worries.

Lilly's (TV) friends are,
Electronic illusions.
Missing in action,
Cause doggy confusion.

Yorkies are yorkies,
And through it all,
So large in love,
In fur, so small.

LA FREEWAY 2011[1]

by

Brian Alan Bild

© 2011

Under siege
Under siege
Oh, my head
Oh, my brain
I'm under siege.

Oh, the cars are coming
They change lanes sprightly
A five lane phalanx
Follows me.

Freeway bound
Cars around.
Cars whiz here
Cars whiz there
Cars, all around.

Like speeding bullets
Move so swiftly.
The world seems
Nothing but a blur.

---

[1] To the tune of "Over There"

Dodge'em cars
Oh, my stars.
Close calls here
Close calls there.
Zig Zag cars.

Harley motorcycles
Careening cycles
They roar as,
Lions of the road.

Jousting knights
Their metal bites.
It's a fight
Free for all,
Wrong or right.

A traffic nightmare
Day and nightmare,
Hard cold metal,
Zooms around.

First you zig
Then you zag.
Faster here,
Faster there,
Then zig zag.

Like NASCAR racers
Sleek car pinballs.
They speed, headlong,
Toward oblivion.

WHAT'S THE THING? (c)

by

Brian Alan Bild

© 2011

What's the thing,
That makes bells ring?
We dedicate,
It motivates.
Count it once.
Count it twice.
Ev'ry cent so.
Heaven sent.

Refrain:
Green's the name,
Yes, it is.
M-O-N-E-Y.

Really great,
'Tis my fate.
Pockets full.
Wonderful.
Money's lent.
Every cent.
More comes in.
It's no sin.

Refrain:

Stack it high,
By and bye.
This desire.
Lights my fire.
Truly mine,
By design.
Money is,
My sole biz.

Refrain:

What I do
For money new.
There's no schism,
I'm money driven.
A money guy
I multiply.
The amount
In my account.

Refrain:

INTO THE FIRE OF SEPTEMBER 11, 2001 (c)

by

Brian Alan Bild

© 2011

They heard the call
That brought them all.
To fight against
Fire's pestilence.

They did begin
Quickly rush in.
The honor of their cause
Righteous just because.

Rush into the fire
A dedicated desire.
'Twas not a trick
Rush to the thick

Pushing smoke away
Trying to save the day.
They were committed
By flames outwitted.

Thus, did multiply,
Their 340 to the sky.
Their number swelled,
Many more were felled.

Hunting for terrorists
Looking for conquests.
Heroes in their minds
Such was their design.

What accomplishment?
To their deaths were sent.
Did we learn, from the fights
Two wrongs don't make a right?

DING DONG DOGGIE

by

Brian Alan Bild

© 2011

I'm a ding, dong, doggie,
From Abilene.
A rootin' tootin' cowboy,
From the Western scene.

See my chaps,
See my spurs.
I keep the peace,
With doggie curs.

I help the sheriff,
He does the job.
We keep things safe,
From doggie mobs.

Watchful waiting's,
Part of the game.
Guns in hand,
We like things tame.

Drunks and ruffians,
I'll calm them down.
Our vigilance,
Let's peace abound.

We watch over widows,
And orphans too.
Protecting the village,
From the bad guy zoo.

STRANGE IS THE LAND I VISIT AND SEE (c)

by

Brian Alan Bild

© 2011

I am a stranger in a strange land
Built by a different mind and hand.
Different values, different things,
Going back to the time of Ming.

Strange, strange, are the things I see,
Built for someone else, not for me.
Is this real or fantasy,
The wonders of the world I see?

What is real to me?
I don't know what I see.
What will it be?
Will it help or hinder me?

Pieces of reality.
What will it be?
Jumbled in my mind.
What will I find?

CHRISTMAS TIME

by

Brian Alan Bild

© 2011

At a time before Christmas,
My mother said to me,
"See the sun, moon and stars.
The best things in life are free."

My father was a banker
His words were family lore:
"The best things in life, my son,
Cost a bit more."

He'd say, "See all those shoppers,
At happy Christmas time.
They know my little secret,
Spending dollars and their dimes."

Buying this, buying that
Wanting more and more.
Competition or addiction?
More of MINE than before.

AN UNSPOKEN COURTHOUSE CREED (c)

by

Brian Alan Bild

© 2011

A distinguished jurist once said.
As he thought and scratched his head:

Justice is precious, precious indeed.
Why waste it on people in need?

Justice so pure and holy,
Given to all, would be folly.

Seeing it every day,
Justice would wither away.

Like soup for too many,
Not worth a penny.

To justice we bow down,
Too precious, to pass around.

Justice is a distant goal,
Because…..justice has no soul.

LOVE AT A DISTANCE

by

Brian Alan Bild

© 2012

Love from a distance,
Is most pure.
So much easier,
That's for sure.

All is harmony,
In love far away.
Everything's bright,
As a sunny day.

The idea of love,
Is most compelling.
Easier telling,
Than daily dwelling.

Thoughts of love,
Can be divine.
Companionship,
Of heart and mind.

99 TO 1

by

Brian Alan Bild

© 2012

Look in your wallet.
Look in your purse.
There you will find,
The results of a curse.

Money's not there.
For some, not a dime.
The RICH want it all.
It's no theft, or crime.

The game is rigged,
By those at the top.
They get the money,
You get the slop.

Torrents of money,
For the one percent.
Others find pennies,
And must be content.

Politics is broken,
Has been for years.
Billions, to one percent
99 have their tears.

Broken, broken,
Broke as can be.
The voters broke it.
Politics ain't free.

Opportunities lost,
99 fall down.
1 per cent victors
99 percent clowns.

Money talks,
Loudest now.
Lemmings will follow,
Asking, How? How? How?

Looking back,
The worst is to come.
Darkness gets deeper
Unless something's done.

Poisoned propaganda
Do you care?
To stop the one percent,
Have you done your share?

You vote them in,
You vote them out.
You have the power,
You have the clout.

Bill Moyers inspires
What can it be?
Poetic, economics,
And life ain't so free.

RAIN, SOME SUN

by

Brian Alan Bild

© 2012

The Northwest is calling.
"Come to me. Come to me.
I scramble life, a new way.
I do things diff'rently."

The weather's rainy,
Almost always; just a bit.
The Northwest is another place,
Your old life to forget.

It's the weather, the weather,
Drizzle here, drizzle there.
Rain gear is essential,
Without it you won't dare.

Renewed like flowers,
Such a saving grace,
From bone chilling cold,
Blowing in your face.

Disheveled is the life,
Protected from rain.
Maybe, it won't rain,
And then, it rains again (and again).

Grunge is the fashion
Because of the rain
Don't be too particular,
And sane, you'll remain.

Out of doors is the life.
Athletic you'll be,
Dodging all those raindrops
Amid flowers and the trees.

FETCH, FLOYD, FETCH!

by

Brian Alan Bild

© 2012

Oh, what a greeting,
Excited! Excited!
The joy of friendship,
That he provided.

Fetch Floyd, fetch!
(Tennis) ball retriever.
Back with a smile,
To his receiver.

Roll him over,
Scratch his tummy.
Tummy enjoyment,
That's Floyd Funky.

Stare down a moose,
He can stop it.
Fearless Floyd
He will do it.

Quietly lovable,
That was Floyd.
Constant companion,
My lovable Floyd.

My doggie tricks,
Are in demand.
Mama's voice,
Is my command.

Good dog! Good dog!
Funky Floyd.
Yes, the good times
We enjoyed.

LEADING ONWARD[1]

by

Brian Alan Bild

© 2012

"Give me your tired, your poor,
Your huddled masses,
Yearning to be free."[2]

America! Land of opportunity.
For soldiers on the ground,
Platitudes in their heads.

To follow leaders so they said,
(G.W.) Bush, Cheney and Rumsfeld,
War mongering draft dodgers aren't dead.

A wider circle of death ahead,
For destruction and wasted trillions of dollars,
Glorifying death/destruction for others.

Horrified are mothers
Soldiers risking life and limb,
Soldiers who can't see.

---

[1] Unusual rhyme scheme

[2] Emma Lazarus

Haunted by PTSD,
Seeing flashbacks
Rerunning horrors in the mind.

Their peace they do not find,
Repeating scenes, no one should see,
Forgotten are the milit'ry.

What is our freedom to be?
Freedom to invade and occupy,
Whatever country we desire.

Killings burn the pyre,
Protecting more oil than freedom.
Truth remains a casualty.

Fight for freedom can you see?
The freedom for oil to flow.
Mangled bodies lubricate the lifestyle.

The million dollar mile,
Per year, per soldier, for a decade,
Napoleon would be proud.

So it goes around.
A Department of Defense
Unresponsive to its name.

POLITICS AS POETRY

by

Brian Alan Bild

© 2012

Many are the times,
In a political life;
Of days brim full,
With political strife.

The phones! The phones!
Are a distraction.
Callers demanding,
Their course of action.

Astute politicians,
Must count votes,
To avoid a sleeper,
Who gets your goat.

Constantly trading;
Votes of this and that.
Lobbyists' meals,
Will make you fat.

"Righteous is my cause"
The voters' hue and cry,
"Ignore the other side.
Please meet my guy."

Helping people,
Some in need.
Nevertheless,
Others in greed.

There's nothing worse,
Than a raucous causus,
We can't agree,
None of us.

Talk, talk, talk,
At times all talk.
What's getting done?...
Oh, for a quiet walk.

Legislative business;
Away from family.
Gone so many days,
Is no way to be.

You can't win them all.
Today it's their way.
We'll do it again.
And, win another day.

The telephone's an enemy,
Calling: Justice! Liberty!
Sanctimonious screaming
Is not my cup of tea.

Everything's so important
Rushing here, rushing there.
Beware of political spies,
With prying eyes and ears.

Sometimes you think,
They're paid by the word.
Repeating so much,
You've already heard.

Proposals, suggestions,
To meet *their* end,
They butter you up.
You're everybody's friend.

Roll call votes
Are such a pain.
They seem to happen
Again, and again, and again.

Parading protesters,
Seem like a mob.
It seems so strange,
I love this job.

STORMS AHEAD

by

Brian Alan Bild

© 2012

Unforgettable,
In many ways.
So impossible,
In many ways.

Unforgettable,
And impossible.
A combination,
Not so wonderful.

Nicknamed stormy,
Fitting name.
Always stormy,
Never the same.

Riding the storm,
Consumes energy.
A mind exhausted,
Is no way to be.

Please be careful,
Don't get hurt.
Too hot to handle,
Might get burnt.

A mind of two minds,
Is not consoled.
A mind of two minds,
Can not be bold.

Storms within,
And storms without.
Dizzy is the man.
Tossed with doubt.

GYPSY MOODS

by

Brian Alan Bild

© 2012

My lady has a gypsy heart,
That wanders to and fro.
What is her inclination?
Such, is where she'll go.

Her heart flits here and there,
What'er her feelings be.
Like a spinning bottle,
Sometimes it points to me.

Sometimes distant, sometimes close,
She does what'er she does.
Can I predict her disposition?
Good gracious heaven knows!

False starts and implications,
Haunt both, her and me.
What kind of journey is this
Flitting, flower to tree?

Constancy of manner,
Is a man's delight.
To please his lady love,
All the days and nights.

Happy is the couple,
Who live in harmony,
They love each other,
What'er the mood might be.

SPINELESS LITTLE WORMS

by

Brian Alan Bild

© 2012

Complain and criticize,
You spineless little worms,
Never remembering;
Hard work has charms.

Glib and thoughtless answers,
You spineless little worms.
Critical thoughts,
Avoid needless harms.

Seek the essentials,
You spineless little worms.
Success will welcome,
With open arms.

Be patient my friends,
You spineless little worms.
The searching eyes of time,
Will make their amends.

Avoiding hard facts,
You spineless little worms.
Factual analysis,
Reduces alarms.

Logic; twisted, distorted,
You spineless little worms.
Eventually the truth wins out,
Despite the vermin's terms.

LOVELY ILLUSIONS

by

Brian Alan Bild

© 2012

I love illusions,
I live in them.
I think of politics,
Without illusions I'll win.

Al Gore came by, one day,
I told him, "Never mind."
"No matter what you say, (he said)
I'm not the losing kind."

Afraid to cross the Rubicon,
Afraid to have a fight.
Within my white castle,
There is no need to fight.

Was it Caesar, who once said,
"Campaigning isn't fun."
"You don't lose a campaign.
If you don't have one."

WHEN HORSES RUN WILD

by

Brian Alan Bild

© 2012

Animals! Beware!
Get out of the way!
Wild horses are coming,
Their hoofs pounding clay.

When horses run wild,
Their hoofs are thunder.
Behind them leaving,
Destruction and plunder.

Wild horses, wild horses,
With headstrong ways.
They run wherever,
For days and days.

The beauty of strength,
The beauty of power.
Run real fast,
And be no coward.

A triumph of strength,
No rider, no reins.
The power, the speed,
Running for gain.

The herd has the power,
They snort and they wheeze.
Wild horses run,
Run as they please.

Horse without rider,
Has nowhere gone.
As if in circles,
Running since dawn.

The horses lead on,
Run fast, run on.
Despite the effort,
Where have they gone?

CROTCH ROCKET

by

Brian Alan Bild

© 2012

Riding my crotch rocket,
Accelerate and go.
Faster than anything,
Rocket's the best show.

From a standing start,
The tires squeal.
Speed's the thing,
The rocket's real.

Pealing rubber; I'm off,
I'm fast, fast, fast.
No one can catch me,
Rock' riding's a blast.

I'm the fastest,
Thing on wheels.
It's amazing,
This thing is lee……gal.

THE LOVE OF MOM AND DAD

by

Brian Alan Bild

© 2012

A mother's love, is first love,
Her kindness nurtured me.
Her quiet loving nature,
Formed, what I would be.

An infant young and helpless,
Lives by parent love.
Caring with compassion,
Is what a parent does.

For the blessings of life,
Thank mother and father.
For decades of patience,
In times of meander.

Through peril and darkness,
Parent love lights the way.
Through a lifetime of living,
No matter; come what may.

BABY BLUE EYES (c)

by

Brian Alan Bild

© 2012

Hypnotized, hypnotized, hypnotized.
So truly hypnotized.
Silent though you are
I could see from afar.
Those baby blue eyes
Couldn't tell lies.
Your baby blue eyes,
Yes, those baby blue eyes.

Decades from now
Men will scrape and bow.
Men will pay their dues
For your beautiful baby blues.
Treat them ever so kindly
As they follow you blindly.
They know not what they do
Seeing your beautiful baby blues.

May your wonderful eyes
Always hypnotize,
Others as open and true
In whatever they do.
Seeing kindness everywhere
May your baby blues dare,
To make grownups gentle
And sentimental.

MIND OVER MOUTH (c)

by

Brian Alan Bild

© 2012

Use your mind, for thoughts old or new.
Your mind is quiet, thoughtful and true
Thoughts are honest, fresh as the dew.
Without thoughts, how would you do?

Quietly think, to know what's new,
Thoughtless words might make you blue.
Discover mistakes, before others do.
With thoughts, mistakes will be few(er).

Banish brainless bubbles anew.
Thoughts, repair themselves for you.
Those thoughts, think them through.
Without thoughts, how would you do?

After smoothing the edges
And completing your pledges
Close the gap.
Relax, take a nap.
(May your thoughts be with you.)

CANDY WRAPPERS (c)

by

Brian Alan Bild

© 2012

Once upon a time
Almost by design.
My tummy said to me
I'm a bit hungry.
I thought about what food
Would put me in the mood.
I'm compelled to eat
Something for a treat.

How about a sweet?
Something sweet to eat.
Now might be the time
Now would be just fine.
What would it be
To set my hunger free,
And not be locked in me?
Just what could it be?

I looked and looked around
Nothing to be found.
Then I spied a sign
For what I need to find.
There across the room
Something to eat soon.
That might do the trick
If I act real quick.

How did I know?
The wrapper told me so.
The wrapper was a tease
To feel what I please.
The wrapper wasn't sweet
It's nothing meant to eat.
Thought it was a clue
For something I might do.

This time a clue it was
For something that one does.
My clue to eat
So I took a seat.
I did sit and sigh
My, oh my, oh my.
Would I find,
What was on my mind?

Are wrappers what I eat?
Not such a crazy feat.
The essence of it all
I hear the candy call.
The candy is for me
In my tummy it should be.
Now I feel contented
My hunger's not lamented.

SEA OF WAVES

by

Brian Alan Bild

© 2012

Onward we roll,
As waves of the sea.
Through cycles and changes,
What will we be?

Seemingly, perpetual;
Always there but changing,
Peaks and valleys all around;
Always, rearranging.

Beneath the surface,
Creatures abound.
Prowling and swimming
Forward and around.

Wonderous waves,
Move and reform.
Motion continues,
New waves formed.

Waves do their dancing.
At sea or at shore.
They fill the horizon,
Those waves evermore.

Always and ever,
'Til waves reach the shore.
Time seems endless,
'Til we reach that shore.

Renewed, refreshed, remade,
Ever in motion, ever grand.
The shore spreads everywhere
Infinite as dunes of sand.

THE TUNNEL (c)

by

Brian Alan Bild

© 2013

Tunnel vision, tunnel vision
I implore you:

A thing simple minds can bear,
The shortest route to anywhere.
I confuse the forest for the trees
Ignoring wasps and honey bees.

Nothing round me to distract me
Keeps life simple as can be.
Can't keep my far from near
The straight and narrow, oh so dear.

It isn't fair, it isn't fair
What could fall from thin air?
Let complications bother others
While I live within my druthers.

I confuse the forest for the trees
Ignoring wasps and honey bees.
Tunnel vision is, so clear to me,
The shortest route from A to B.

DRONING ON AND ON (c)

by

Brian Alan Bild

© 2013

Once upon a time
A politician, turned on a dime.
His droning words of hope,
Comfort only now a dope.

When black revenge begins its creep,
Blackness is, more than skin deep.
If, black purpose preceded,
Black shirts, brown shirts not needed.

Rumsfeld by another name.
Needless death just the same.
The Inferno needs a new circle,
For those with the power of purple.

The investment bankers' wimp
Is now the violence pimp.
Has the peace prize holder
Become infinitely bolder?

An assassin's blood-soaked finger
Points to the sky borne stinger.
His education stoops so low
When morality, it does not know.

He is the judge, the jury,
Drone death is his fury.
Collateral damage all around
Within the kill zone, it abounds.

Innocents to the slaughter
The young sons and daughters.
He cares when school children die,
If, American apple pie.

With Chicago mafia style
Words do not beguile.
Anger drowns morality,
Ignoring all reality.

Words from this constitutional scholar
Aren't worth a dime or a dollar.
Kind words are just for fun
His enemies zig-zag and run.

His finger drips of blood,
As dead drop in the mud.
Never learned an Abu Grab lesson
With Mighty Finger you're a messin'.

What would (our) founding fathers think?
They would raise a deathly stink.
While Congress sits and squats,
Full destruction we have got.

Drones are the weapon of choice
Tiny groundlings have no voice.
Get on your knees and pray
For light of a better day.

His hope has no meaning
In actions demeaning.
Is a warring President,
Best with his conscience cut out?

Without compassionate feats
Life becomes mean streets.
Their loss of humanity
Is our loss of humanity.

Our critics may have been right
About America's might:
Does America lead the way
As the land of moral decay?

CARRY THE CANDLE

by

Brian Alan Bild

© 2013

As others have done before me;
I can light the candle,
Carry it wherever I go.
I can light the path,
My candle will lighten the load.
I can <u>not</u> forever carry the candle
Others must continue to lighten the load.
Wherever you go, carry the candle,
Carry the candle wherever you go.

MY ROAD LESS TRAVELED (c)

by

Brian Alan Bild

© 2013

I too saw roads ahead,
They were two roads, as said,
One was traveled, straight and plain
The other turned and turned again.

I too, took the second road: less traveled,
Along that road for years I marveled,
Soaking in what was to be
Like a human honey bee.

Slowly putting pieces in place,
Growth in happiness, love and grace.
Decade after decade, I could understand
Life was tough. Life was grand.

At last expressing my days,
Of life's many, changing ways.